LOST TRAMWAYS OF ENGLAND
LONDON NORTH-WEST

PETER WALLER

GRAFFEG

CONTENTS

LONDON NORTH-WEST

1. Farringdon Street
2. Smithfield
3. Aldersgate
4. Moorgate
5. Angel, Islington
6. Grays Inn Road
7. Stamford Hill
8. Bloomsbury
9. Holloway
10. Highgate Village
11. Kentish Town
12. Parliament Hill Fields

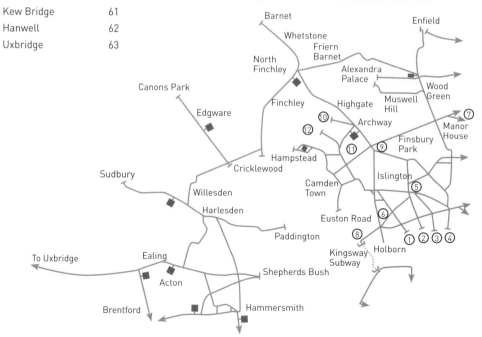

INTRODUCTION

Although there had been street tramways in Britain from the early 1860s in places like Birkenhead and London, it was not until the 1870 Tramways Act that a legislative framework was established for their construction and operation. The Act empowered local authorities to grant licences to companies to operate tramways for a 21-year period. The licensee could construct the tramway itself or the route could be constructed by the local authority and leased as part of the franchise to the operator. Initially, it was expected that private companies would always operate the tramways built; however, in 1883, Huddersfield Corporation in the West Riding of Yorkshire, having constructed a new steam tramway to serve the town, was unable to find a licensee willing to take on operation and so became the first municipal operator of trams within the British Isles.

The 1870 Act imposed a number of restrictions upon the tramway builder and operator; with the benefit of hindsight, it can be seen that these had a negative impact upon tramway development in the United Kingdom and undoubtedly represented one factor in the demise of the tramcar from the 1920s onwards. One of these clauses required the builder and operator of the tramway to maintain the public highway to a distance of 18 inches outside each running line; this effectively made the tramway owner responsible for the upkeep of the road surface on those streets where trams operated. At a time when the condition of the public highway was often poor, the well-built and well-maintained section over which the trams operated became a magnet for other road users. As road traffic increased, so trams – despite the fact that the road had been constructed to accommodate them – were increasingly perceived as a cause of road traffic delays.

The second weakness within the 1870 Act was the so-called 'scrap iron clause'; this permitted the licensor – usually the local authority – to take over the assets (such as the trams) owned by the licensee at asset value – including depreciation – rather than reflecting the value of the business. As a result, tramway licensees became increasingly unwilling to invest in their business as the licence period came towards its end. The Act permitted the termination of the licence after 21 years and every seven years thereafter. For company-owned operations this sword of Damocles meant that the threat of municipalisation was ever present and, even if never exercised, was sufficient to ensure that modernisation might never take place. The classic example here is the tramways of Bristol; operated throughout their career by a company but with the constant threat of take-over by Bristol Corporation, the system survived through until 1941 operating open-top and unvestibuled trams that would not have been out of place on the first electric tramways built at the end of the 19th century whereas other systems were operating state-of-the-art modern trams by World War II.

This volume is one of a series that cover the tramways of England and is one of four looking at the tramways of London. This volume examines the history of the tramways that operated on the north-west side of the Thames.

London County Council

The LCC electric network in north-west London comprised a number of routes that had their origins in horse tramways along with extensions beyond the horse tram network. In addition, there was a short cable tramway that served Highgate Hill.

The first electric trams to serve the area were those on the section that involved the Kingsway Subway and covered the route from Aldwych to the Angel Islington; this opened on 24 February 1906. The subway was extended south from Aldwych to the Embankment on 10 April 1908.

North from the Angel to Highbury Corner opened on 16 November 1906. This was followed by the line from Theobalds Road (Bloomsbury) eastwards to Gardiner's Corner; this section opened on 16 January 1907. The lower end of Grays Inn Road to the terminus at Holborn opened on the same day. Further sections to open during 1907 were along St John Street to the terminus at Smithfield, along Pentonville Road and City Road (all on 29 July), to be followed on 27 November by the section along Goswell Road and on 5 December by the northern section of

Grays Inn Road. Grays Inn Road was connected to Caledonian Road, following the reconstruction of the railway bridge, on 1 June 1912. The route along Holloway Road to the Archway Tavern opened on 18 December 1907.

The route from Brook Green Lane (Hammersmith) to Scrubs Lane (Harlesden) opened on 30 May 1908; this was planned as part of a route linked through to services south of the river. On 23 January 1909 the route from Hammersmith to Putney opened, but it was not until 30 January 1912, with the opening of a connection in Hammersmith Broadway, that the two parts of the route were united.

The section from Holloway Road to Finsbury Park station along Seven Sisters Road opened on 9 July 1908; a connection was made with the MET at Finsbury Park but through running was impossible, as the LCC section used conduit. The Caledonian Road section to Seven Sisters Road opened on 15 August 1908. This was followed on 31 July 1909 by the opening of the section from Islington Green to Essex Road.

The route from the Nags Head along Parkhurst Road and Camden Road to Camden Town station opened on 11 April 1909; it was extended south to a new terminus at Euston on 29 May 1909. Also on 29 May, the section along King's Cross Road and Farringdon Road as far as Clerkenwell Road was opened. This was extended through to a new terminus at Farringdon Street on 14 May 1910. The section from King's Cross to Camden Town via Pancras Road and Crowndale Road opened on 22 July 1909. On 10 September 1909 electric trams were introduced to the section along Great College Street and Prince of Wales Road; this was followed on 30 November 1909 by the lines to Hampstead via Chalk Farm Road and Ferdinand Street and Fortess Road and Junction Road.

The Highgate Hill route was the next to be opened; this line from Archway had been cable operated – a consequence of the 1 in 11 gradient – and electrification required the use of special brakes on the tram used. The route reopened, after conversion, on 25 March 1910. This was followed on 20 May 1911 by the opening of the section up Highgate Road as far as Parliament Hill Fields.

The section from Manor House south to New North Road opened in two stages: on 22 November 1912 from Manor House to Balls Pond Road and thence to New North Road four days later. This work included a single line spur westwards along Balls Pond Road, also opened on 26 November 1912. The connection with the tramway along Essex Road was further improved in early 1913 with the opening on 25 July with the single track along Dorset Street. The section linking Highbury Corner with City Road via Holloway Road, Canonbury Road and New North Road opened on 25 June 1914.

The complex arrangement at Manor House and Finsbury Park was simplified when the LCC took over certain sections of the already electrified MET and converted them to conduit operation (although the Manor House to Finsbury Park section retained overhead as well). LCC services were extended from Finsbury Park to Manor House in 1915.

After World War I, the section along Amhurst Park opened on 31 March 1924. Apart from the reconstruction of various junctions thereafter, this was the last significant addition to the tramway network north of the river.

London United Tramways

The bulk of the LUT network was located in south-west London and Surrey, but certain sections are dealt with in this volume. On 4 April 1901, the sections from Hammersmith to Kew Bridge and Shepherds Bush to both Young's Corner and Acton were opened. On 10 July the Acton service was extended to Southall. On 1 June 1904, two sections opened; these were from Southall to Uxbridge and Studland Street to the Askew Arms. Finally, there was the route linking Hanwell with Brentford via Boston Road; this opened on 26 May 1906. The track around Hammersmith and Shepherd's Bush was located within the LCC area and was transferred to the LCC after World War I, although the LUT continued to operate the relevant routes.

Metropolitan Electric Tramways

MET was established to take over and electrify an existing network of horse and steam tramways that operated in north and north-west London, largely in the area controlled by Middlesex County Council. When it was first established, it was a subsidiary of British Electric Traction Ltd, but it eventually became part of the London & Suburban

Traction Co Ltd in 1913; this was a company jointly owned by BET and by the Underground Electric Railways Co.

The first two sections – from Finsbury Park to Wood Green and from Manor House east along Seven Sisters Road to Seven Sisters Corner – opened on 22 July 1904. These were followed on 20 August 1904 by the section from Wood Green to Bruce Grove and on 24 August 1904 by that from Seven Sisters Corner northwards to Brantwood Road; the latter was extended the short distance to the boundary between Edmonton and Tottenham during October 1904. The section from Cricklewood to Edgware via Hendon was the last extension in 1904 when it opened on 3 December.

Two sections – from Seven Sisters Road to Tottenham and from the Edmonton boundary to Angel Bridge – on 12 April 1905. This was followed on 7 June 1905 by the opening of the route from Archway to Whetstone and, on 19 July 1905, by the line from Angel Bridge to Tramway Avenue. There were two further extensions during 1905. The first of these, on 6 December, saw the opening of the first route to Alexandra Palace, from the Wellington (Turnpike Lane) via

Muswell Hill, and, on 22 December, the link from Highgate Archway to the Archway Tavern.

On 31 March 1906 the route between Cricklewood and Willesden Green station was opened, to be followed, on 11 April, by the opening of the connection between Bruce Grove and Tottenham and the second route to Alexandra Palace (from Wood Green). Later in the year – on 4 August – the Whetstone route was extended through to the boundary with Hertfordshire; this was extended through to Barnet on 28 March 1907. The section from Harlesden to Stonebridge Park opened on 10 October 1906. The Wood Green to Bounds Green section opened on 28 October 1906 (extended to New Southgate station on 10 May 1907) and the final opening that year, on 22 December, was from Harlesden to Lock Hospital Bridge.

The Wood Green service was extended to Palmers Green on 7 June 1907 whilst the Edgware service was extended to Canons Park on 31 October 1907. The Tramway Avenue service was extended northwards to the boundary between Middlesex and Hertfordshire on 11 December 1907 – this was tended through to Waltham Cross on 17 April

1908 – whilst the Willesden Green station service was extended through to Cravens Park, where it connected into the service to Stonebridge Park, on 23 December 1907.

The Stonebridge Park service was extended to Wembley on 15 April 1908; this was further extended through to Sudbury on 24 September 1910. The section from Harlesden to Willesden Junction station opened on 30 June 1908; this was extended through to Acton on 8 October 1909. The Palmers Green to Winchmore Hill section opened on 1 August 1908; this was extended through to Enfield on 3 July 1909.

On 8 April 1909 the route to New Southgate was extended to North Finchley and the section from North Finchley to Golders Green opened on 17 December 1909; this was further extended to Cricklewood on 21 February 1910 (this included a short stub terminus at Childs Hill).

The route from Lock Hospital Bridge to a new terminus at Paddington opened in two stages: to Warwick Avenue on 14 July 1910 and thence to Paddington itself on 6 December 1910. The MET's final extension – from Ponders End to Enfield – opened on 20 February 1911.

During the years after World War I the MET's relationships with its landlords – most notably Middlesex County Council – were not always harmonious, largely as a result of declining maintenance standards, but investment later in the 1920s and the purchase of the 'Felthams' meant that the MET system was in a better position in 1933 than it had been a decade earlier.

The LPTB takes over

On 1 July 1933 the LPTB took over operation of all the tramways within London; for the first time, the entire network was under the control of a single body.

In terms of north-west London, the single largest element inherited by the LPTB was contributed by the LCC. In all, throughout London, the LCC operated over almost 158 route miles with a fleet of 1,663 trams. These were accommodated in 16 depots. In addition to operating over its own track, the LCC had also negotiated through-running agreements with all the tramways into which it connected with the exception of Erith in south-east London. The fleet had been modernised during the late 1920s and more than 300 new trams had also been acquired between 1929 and 1932.

The only operator to run exclusively in north-west London was the MET; this was the largest of the three companies to operate electric tramways in the metropolis. It ran over a network of 53¾ route miles, although it actually owned just over 9½ route miles – the rest was leased from Middlesex and Hertfordshire county councils. It owned a fleet of 316 trams; of these, the vast majority were elderly – albeit upgraded – but it did include 54 of the production 'Feltham' cars completed in 1930/31.

The LUT was the primary operator of trams in the south-west of London and into Surrey; in terms of the area covered by this volume, it operated westwards from Shepherds Bush and Hammersmith to Brentford, Hanwell and Uxbridge. The LUT had already instituted a programme of tram-to-trolleybus conversion and this was to influence the future strategy of the LPTB. The LUT also possessed a fleet dominated by elderly – but modernised – trams, supplemented by 46 of the 'Feltham' type.

The trolleybuses arrive

In July 1934 the LPTB obtained the Royal Assent for its first powers to convert the tramway network to trolleybus operation; further Acts followed annually between then and 1939. The scale of the potential conversion was immense: at the end of June 1934 the LPTB operated a tramway network of 324 route miles with a fleet of 2,560 trams – by far the largest in the British Isles.

The initial conversions continued the gradual elimination of the ex-LUT network in south-west London as well as the bulk of the South Met system around Croydon. It was another ex-LUT route – the 89 from Hammersmith to Acton – which was the first route covered in this volume to be converted when it became trolleybus service 660 on 5 April 1936. This was followed on 5 July 1936 by the first conversions to affect the ex-MET network when routes 66 (Acton to Canons Park) and 68 (Acton to Harlesden) – plus existing trolleybus service 660 – were replaced by trolleybuses on route 666, with buses being used on the section from Edgware to Canons Park.

The next conversions occurred on 2 August 1936, when routes 45 (Cricklewood to North Finchley via Golders Green) and 60 (Paddington to North Finchley via Harlesden and Golders Green) were replaced by trolleybus services 645 and new 660 respectively. These were followed on 23 August 1936 by the conversion of routes 62 (Paddington to Sudbury) and 64 (Paddington to Cricklewood and Edgware) to trolleybus operation as routes 662 and 664.

The last of the inherited ex-LUT network to be converted took place on two dates – on 15 November 1936 and 13 December 1936 respectively – with the conversion of routes 7 (Shepherds Bush to Uxbridge) and 55 (Hanwell to Brentford) by trolleybus services 607 and 655; the latter was extended from Brentford to Hammersmith at the same time.

The next services to be closed were those that served Alexandra Palace (on 23 February 1938); the 37 from Wood Green was abandoned whilst the 39 and 51, which both served the section from the Wellington to Alexandra Palace via Muswell Hill, were diverted or modified. Both sections were eventually replaced by bus services. These conversions resulted in the final use of single-deck trams in London.

The first of the major tram-to-trolleybus conversions to affect north London occurred on 6 March 1938. Route 9 (Moorgate to North Finchley) was replaced by trolleybus route 609 (which was extended through to serve Barnet); routes 11EX (the Sunday-only service from Essex Road to Highgate Village; this was reinstated on 8 May 1938), 13 (Aldersgate to Highgate), 19 (Tottenham Court Road to Barnet), 51 (Aldersgate to Wood Green) and 71 (Aldersgate to Wood Green) were withdrawn; the 17 (Farringdon Street to Archway Tavern, Highgate) was replaced by trolleybus services 517 and 617; the 27 (Tottenham Court Road to Edmonton) was made a seven-day service; the 35A was replaced by short workings on route 35; the 39 (Bruce Grove to Wood Green) became a seven-day service, with the 39A withdrawn (these services had been modified the previous month); finally, the 41 was extended from Manor House to Winchmore Hill.

These were followed on 8 May 1938 with the conversion of routes 29 (Enfield to Tottenham Court Road), 39 (Bruce Grove to Wood Green) and 41 (Moorgate to Winchmore Hill); these became trolleybus services 629, 625 (extended to run from Bruce Grove to Walthamstow) and 641.

It was the turn of the Hampstead routes to be converted on 10 July 1938. Routes 3 (Holborn to Hampstead) and 7 (Holborn to Parliament Hill Fields) were both replaced by trolleybus services 513 and 613 whilst the 5 (Moorgate to Hampstead) and 15 (Moorgate to Parliament Hill Fields) became trolleybus services 639 and 615 respectively.

The final conversion of routes covered in this volume to trolleybus operation occurred on 10 December 1939, when routes 11 (Moorgate to Highgate Village) and 11X (the peak-hour-only service from Essex Road to Highgate Village) became trolleybus service 611. These routes were converted later than others in the area, as it proved difficult to locate a turning circle at the terminus. As a result of the gradient on Highgate Hill, the replacement trolleybuses were fitted with additional braking.

The end of trams in north London

With the exception of three services that linked north and south London via the Kingsway Subway – the 31 (Islington Green to Battersea), the 33 (Manor House to West Norwood) and the 35 (Highgate to Forest Hill) – the conversion of the entire network in north-west London had now been completed. The remaining services would continue through the war and the immediate post-war years. The announcement in early 1950 that the programme to convert London's last tram routes – 'Operation Tramaway' – was to commence later in that year resulted in the 31 being converted as part of Stage 1 – over the weekend of 30 September/1 October 1950 – whilst, having been delayed from earlier, the final Kingsway Subway routes were finally to be converted as part of Stage 7 over the weekend of 5/6 April 1952. These latter conversions, however, saw the trams replaced by bus rather than trolleybus.

A note on the photographs

The majority of the illustrations in this book have been drawn from the collection of the Online Transport Archive, a UK-registered charity that was set up to accommodate collections put together by transport enthusiasts who wished to see their precious images secured for the long-term. Further information about the archive can be found at: www.onlinetransportarchive.org or email secretary@onlinetransportarchive.org

KINGSWAY SUBWAY

Promoted in the early years of the 20th century, the first section of the Kingsway Subway – from the northern entrance to Aldwych – opened on 24 February 1906, with the southern extension through to link with the existing services along the Embankment following on 10 April 1908. The subway was initially constructed for use by single-deck trams, as demonstrated by this view of 'G' class No 569 descending towards the subway from Southampton Row. In all, there were 50 single-deck trams built for operation through the subway; these comprised the 16 trams – Nos 552-67 – that were built by the United Electric Car Co Ltd, designated Class F, and the 34 – Nos 558-601 – built by Brush, which became Class G. Both types were equipped with Mountain & Gibson bogies and all were new

during late 1905 and 1906. Following the decision to rebuild the subway, all were withdrawn during 1929 and 1930. Whilst the bodies were scrapped, the bogies and other equipment were utilised in the construction of the final batch of 'E/1's – the 'Subway Rebuilds' – Nos 552-601.

When the Kingsway Subway opened to the Embankment in 1908, the junction from the southern portal permitted trams to head either east or west along Victoria Embankment. Prior to the rebuilding of the subway, the north to east curve had been eliminated, with trams using the subway thereafter making use of Westminster Bridge to access the network south of the river. The southern portal – pictured here as a southbound 'E/3' emerges with a service on route 35 – was further altered in 1937 as a result of the construction of the new Waterloo Bridge, which formally opened on 21 November 1937. Following the conversion of routes 33 and 35 in April 1952, the southern portal was closed up by metal doors. Beyond the entrance a section of the subway was incorporated into the new Strand underpass – which opened on 21 January 1964 – but the space between the portal and the underpass was converted into a bar that opened in 2008.

By 1929, the single-deck trams in use on the subway were proving inadequate and it was decided to rebuild it to accommodate double-deck vehicles. As part of the work the subway closed temporarily on 2 February 1930; when reopened on 14 January 1931 – with, appropriately, No 1931 being the first tram to use it – the subway was able to accommodate the new all-metal construction 'E/3' double-deckers. Two underground stations – Holborn and Aldwych – were also altered, and it is at the former that 'E/3' No 187 is pictured in March 1952. Before World War II there were plans for the conversion of the subway to trolleybus operation – indeed, an experimental trolleybus (No 1379) was constructed to demonstrate the possibility – but the conversion programme after the war resulted in the motorbus rather than the trolleybus being the preferred replacement. As a result, following the conversion of the final subway routes in April 1952, the subway was abandoned. The northernmost section, from Aldwych to Southampton Row, remains largely intact.

The northern entrance to the Kingsway Subway was situated on Southampton Row, with the emerging trams then turning east into Theobalds Road before heading towards Grays Inn Road. Pictured ascending the 1 in 10 gradient of the ramp out of the subway is ex-Leyton 'E/3' No 166 heading towards Manor House with a service on route 33. Note the signal lights visible to the left of the tram; these were used to control movements on the gradient. Although the southern end of the subway has been incorporated into the Strand underpass, the northern entrance to the subway remains intact and represents probably the most significant relic of the tramway era in central London; retaining its conduit track, the view today – bar the tram – is remarkably similar to that from 70 years ago. The surviving elements of the subway are now Grade II listed.

BLOOMSBURY

It's 5 April 1952 and the last day of tram services through the Kingsway subway and so the passengers waiting to board 'E/3' No 2001 in Bloomsbury are perhaps making their final journey via a form of transport that they may well have known all their lives. The buildings on Theobalds Road that form the backdrop are still extant – albeit now much rebuilt – and the contemporary scene is dominated by the presence of a bus lane.

Another scene from 5 April 1952 sees the last day of the services operated through the Kingsway Subway as 'HR/2' No 118 makes its way northwards along Rosebery Avenue at the junction with Farringdon Road with a service on route 35 towards Highgate. Heading inbound is 'K2' trolleybus service No 1254 on route 581 towards Bloomsbury. Farringdon Road had been used by tram service 17, from Farringdon Street to Highgate, until it was replaced by trolleybus services 517 and 617 on 6 March 1938. No 118 was one of only three of this batch of 'HR/2s' to survive until this date as, lacking trolleypoles, they were restricted to route 35; the other two were Nos 121 and 122. Nos 118 and 122 were scrapped almost immediately after the conversion, during April 1952, whilst No 121 lingered on until the following month.

For services from north London there were five termini situated on the northside of the City of London; the westernmost of these was at Holborn, and 'E/1' No 1056 is pictured departing from the terminus with a service on route 43 towards Stamford Hill via Shoreditch. In 1934 this was the terminus for six services – the 3, 7, 21, 43 and 59 that operated each day along with the 75 that operated on weekdays only. Trolleybuses replaced trams during 1938 and 1939; the first service to be replaced was the 21, which became trolleybus routes 521 and 621 on 6 March 1938. This was followed on 10 July 1938 by trolleybuses on routes 513 and 613 replacing tram routes 3 and 7. On 16 October 1938 trolleybus route 659 was introduced in place of the 59. Finally, route 43 was converted to trolleybuses – as route 643 – on 5 February 1939; at the same time, route 75 was abandoned without direct replacement (although route 81 services were strengthened between Hackney and Bloomsbury to compensate). No 1056 was one of the 'E/1s' stored during World War II but was scrapped – in November 1945 – once peace was restored and the need for reserve trams to replace war-damaged vehicles had ended.

ALDERSGATE

Pictured awaiting departure from Aldersgate is 'E/1' No 890 with a service on route 77 to West India Docks via Dalston Junction. The 77 was the only daily service that made use of the terminus at Aldersgate in 1934; in addition to this there were two weekday services – the 51 and the 71 – along with two services – the 13 and the 41EX – that operated at peak hours only, demonstrating how significant commuter traffic towards the City of London was. Trams were eliminated from Aldersgate in effectively two stages. The first of these saw the 13 and the 51 withdrawn in connection with the introduction of trolleybus routes 517/21 and 617/21 on 6 March 1938; at the same time, route 71 was withdrawn between Aldersgate and Wood Green. The last route to serve Aldersgate was the 77; this was replaced by trolleybus service 677 on 10 September 1939. However, the lack of a suitable location for a turning circle at Aldersgate saw the 677 terminate at Smithfield.

MOORGATE

Never permitted to penetrate to the heart of the City, London's trams made use of a number of termini situated to the north. One of these was Moorgate, where, on 27 February 1938, 'E/1' No 1074 is pictured awaiting departure with a service towards Barnet. Moorgate was the terminus of no fewer than five daily services – these were the 5 to Hampstead, the 9 to North Finchley, the 11 to Highgate Village, the 19 to Barnet and the 41 to Manor House – along with the weekdays-only service 83 to Stamford Hill. By February 1938, the services to North Finchley and Barnet were approaching the end; they were both replaced by trolleybus service 609 on 6 March 1938. The final tram service to Moorgate – the 11 – became trolleybus service No 611 on 10 December 1939.

THE ANGEL, ISLINGTON

The entire ex-LCC network north of the River Thames was converted to trolleybus operation before World War II except for the sections along the Embankment and through the Kingsway Subway to Highgate Archway on route 35, Islington Green on route 31 and Manor House on route 33. The junction for the routes north of the subway was slightly beyond The Angel, Islington. On 5 April 1952 – the last day of tram services through the subway – 'HR/2' No 121 is seen heading southbound with a service on route 35 towards New Cross Gate as trolleybus No 302 heads northbound on route 609 towards Barnet. No 121 was one of a batch – Nos 101-59 – that was built by Hurst Nelson and delivered during 1931. Designed for use solely on routes equipped with conduit, the batch was never fitted with trolleypoles.

Eight of the batch – Nos 112/23-25/29-31/48 – were destroyed by enemy action during World War II, with No 127 being seriously damaged but rebuilt.

The terminus at Manor House was situated just to the south of the intersection between Seven Sisters Road and Green Lanes. Two daily services – the 33 to West Norwood and the 41 to Moorgate – terminated there, as did the peak-hour service 41EX (to Aldersgate). Pictured at the terminus is 'E/1' class No 1276. This tram, which was one of the type delivered during 1910, was scrapped in February 1939. On 6 March 1938, route 41 was extended northwards to terminate at Winchmore Hill; prior to that date, the extension had been operated during peak hours only. This arrangement was not, however, to last long, as on 8 May 1938, route 41 was converted into trolleybus route 641. The 33 was, however, to survive longer; as one of the Kingsway Subway routes running through to south London, it survived through the war and until

the penultimate stage of 'Operation Tramway' over the weekend of 5/6 April 1952. The conversion of the surviving subway routes had originally been scheduled for earlier in the programme but was postponed as a result of delays in completing the construction of the new bus garage at Stockwell.

SEVEN SISTERS ROAD

On 27 July 1938, as No STL 885, which was new in December 1935, heads westbound along Seven Sisters Road with a service on route 42 to Finsbury Park, 'Subway Rebuild' No 591 heads towards Edmonton Town Hall with a service on route 27. The tracks in the foreground are those along Amhurst Park; this section of track, linking Seven Sisters Road with Stamford Hill, was the last significant extension completed north of the Thames and opened on 31 March 1924. Of the daily services that ran along Seven Sisters Road from Manor House to Tottenham, the 59 and 79 became trolleybus operated as the 659 and 679 on 16 October 1938, whilst the 27 survived a few weeks longer, being replaced by trolleybus service 627 on 6 November 1938. The only service to use Amhurst Park – the 53 – from Aldgate to Tottenham Court Road – became trolleybus operated, as route 653, on 5 March 1939.

The terminus of the Alexandra Palace via Muswell Hill service was situated alongside the Wellington public house at the corner of Turnpike Lane and Green Lanes and it is at this location that one of the Class E single-deckers – No 2313 – is pictured. The pub closed in the 1980s and has subsequently been a branch of Burger King and later Costa Coffee. The MET services 34 (Bruce Grove to Muswell Hill) and 34A (Wellington to Alexandra Palace) were both renumbered route 39 on 3 October 1934. The service from Muswell Hill to Alexandra Palace was seasonal, being suspended during the winter months in later years.

Although undated, this view of ex-MET Class C/1 No 2298 at Wood Green must date to between 1 July 1933, when the LPTB was established, and 3 October 1934, when service 18 from Wood Green to Bruce Grove was renumbered 39A. The 20-strong 'C/1' class – MET Nos 192-211 and LPTB Nos 2282-301 – were delivered with Brush-built open-top bodies during 1908. They were fitted with Mountain & Gibson reversed maximum traction bogies. All were modified by Chiswick Works during 1929 and fitted with fully enclosed upper-deck top covers. Although No 2298 retains its MET livery, all of the batch were subsequently repainted into LPTB red. Withdrawal of the type occurred during 1936 and 1937, with No 2298 being scrapped in August 1936. The Wood Green to Bruce Grove service, latterly renumbered 39, was replaced by trolleybus service 625 on 8 May 1938.

Although the section from Muswell Hill to Alexandra Palace was restricted to single-deck operation only, it was possible to operate two types of double-deck trams, when fitted with top covers, as far as the Muswell Hill terminus of route 51. However, due to a low railway bridge under the East Coast Main Line on Turnpike Lane, this operation was restricted to MET Classes C2 and G as their overall height – 15ft 1¾in – was such to enable them to pass under the bridge. Pictured at Muswell Hill is 'G' class No 2275; all 21 of this type were scrapped between June 1938 and January 1939 and represented the last survivors from the trams inherited by the LPTB from the MET other than the 'Felthams', which were transferred for operation south of the river. The section from the Wellington to Alexandra Palace via Muswell Hill was abandoned on 23 February 1938 with buses replacing the trams.

There were two ex-MET sections that served Alexandra Palace – one from Wood Green and the other via Muswell Hill. The latter ran from the Wellington via Muswell Hill to terminate on the southside of Alexandra Palace itself, and it is at this terminus that 'E' class No 2303 is pictured. The 20-strong 'E' class – MET Nos 131-50 – were built by Brush in 1905 and equipped with the same manufacturer's radial four-wheel trucks. This type were the only single-deck trams owned by MET and were designed for use on the Alexandra Palace lines, as low bridges precluded the use of double-deck trams. Four of the batch were sold to Auckland in New Zealand in 1907 and a fifth passed to LUT in 1922. The surviving cars became LPTB Nos 2302-16 in July 1933. They were to remain in service until the conversion of the services to Alexandra Palace on 23 February 1938.

The second service to Alexandra Palace ran from Wood Green via Station Road to serve the east of the complex. Seen approaching the terminus as a second tram awaits departure with a service towards Wood Green is another of the 'E' class trams – No 2306 – which had originally been MET No 138 when new in 1905. The section from Wood Green to Alexandra Palace East was abandoned in favour of replacement buses on 23 February 1938.

WINCHMORE HILL

Following the conversions of 6 March 1938, route 41, which had previously terminated at Manor House, was extended to Winchmore Hill, which had previously only been served by the 41 during peak hours only. This was, however, only a short-term measure, as the route was amongst those converted to trolleybus operation – as route 641 – on 8 May 1938. With the trolleybus overhead already in place, 'E/1' No 1121 is pictured at the Winchmore Hill terminus shortly before the route's conversion. No 1121 was one of the batch built by Hurst Nelson during 1908 and 1909; it was to survive the conversion of the 41 but was scrapped in June the following year.

ENFIELD

There were two termini in Enfield: on
London Road and on Southbury Road.
Pictured at the former with a service
on route 29 towards Tottenham Court
Road is Class G No 2264 (ex-MET No
219). The 29 was the only daily service
to Enfield; it was supplemented in peak
hours by the 39A from Bruce Grove,
a service that normally terminated at
Wood Green. The latter had been MET
service 18 until a number of routes
were renumbered in October 1934.
All tram services to Enfield (London
Road) were replaced by trolleybuses
on 8 May 1938. No 2264 was to survive
the conversion of the 29, not being
scrapped until January 1939.

TOTTENHAM COURT ROAD

The terminus close to Euston station was situated at the junction of Euston Road and Tottenham Court Road, with trams heading northbound from the terminus up Hampstead Road. The terminus was used by three daily services – the 19 to Barnet, the 29 to Enfield and the 53 to Aldgate – plus one weekdays-only service (the 27 to Edmonton), one weekday peak-hour-only service (the 25 to Parliament Hill Fields) and special service 1 (a Whitsun and August bank holiday service to Hampstead). The 29 was a haunt, following its introduction, of the 'Feltham' type, and here No 2076 awaits departure with a service towards Enfield. Following extensive development work during the 1920s, which saw a number of experimental trams constructed, the MET took delivery of 54 of the production cars, built by the Union Construction & Finance Co (of Feltham), with the LUT taking a further 46. The acquisition of the 'Feltham' cars by the LUT and the MET reflected a commitment on the part of both operators for the retention of trams on their trunk services but the creation of the LPTB, with its determination to eliminate the trams, negated these aspirations. No 2076 had originally been MET No 332. Like the remainder of the type, No 2076 was transferred south of the river following the conversion programme; the last route in north London to be operated by the type was the 29, which was to become trolleybus service 629 on 8 May 1938. Withdrawn in September 1950, No 2076 was sold to Leeds Corporation, where, as No 524, it entered service in February 1951. Withdrawn for the second time in October 1958, it was scrapped in April 1959.

In 1938, 'E' class No 608 is pictured about to turn right from Prince of Wales Road into Kentish Town Road with a service on route 3 from Hampstead to Holborn. This service was one of the two daily services that operated to Hampstead; the other was the 5 that operated through to Moorgate. These were replaced by trolleybuses, operating on routes 513 and 639 respectively, on 10 July 1938 and evidence of the imminent conversion can be seen in the new trolleybus overhead. No 608 was withdrawn following these conversions and was scrapped in August 1938.

HAMPSTEAD

The terminus of routes 3 (to Moorgate) and 5 (to Holborn) was situated at the end of single-track sections: outbound trams operated along Fleet Road whilst inbound trams took Agincourt Road, with Hampstead depot situated between the two. Pictured in 1938 – shortly before the conversion of the routes in July that year (as evinced by the newly installed trolleybus overhead) – at the terminus alongside a third tram on route 5 are two trams – 'E' class No 537 and 'E/1' No 552 (the first numerically of the 'Subway Rebuilds') – on the Holborn service. A total of 300 'E' class trams – Nos 402-551 and 602-751 – were built by Hurst Nelson in 1906 and were fitted with Mountain & Gibson maximum-traction bogies. Equipped with fully-enclosed upper decks from new, only Nos 402-511 were fitted with trolleypoles, with the remainder being conduit-operation only. All of the type – with the exception of No 420 (which had been rebuilt following an accident in the early 1930s and renumbered as 'E/'1 No 1597 in the late 1930s) – were withdrawn during the period from 1936 to 1938, with No 537 being scrapped in August 1938.

PARLIAMENT HILL FIELDS

Two daily services operated to the terminus at Parliament Hill Fields on Highgate Road; these were the 7 to Holborn and the 15 to Moorgate and, on 10 April 1938, 'Subway Rebuild' Class E/1 No 580 is pictured on the former whilst 'E' class No 543 prepares to depart on the latter. The driver is watching carefully as two passengers make a dash for No 543, obviously oblivious to the fact that the crew has posed in front of the tram. The two services were replaced by trolleybus route 613 and 615 respectively on 10 July 1938. Although No 580 was to survive the war, No 543 was a casualty of the July 1938 conversions and was scrapped the following month.

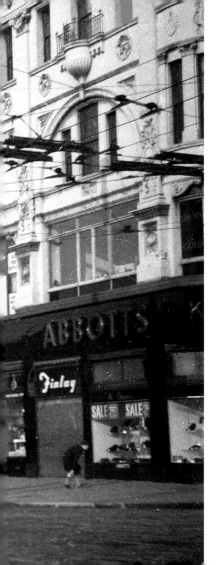

HOLLOWAY ROAD

As 'J1' class trolleybus No 910 passes on the nearside with an inbound service on route 609 towards Moorgate, a tram makes its way southbound at the Nag's Head, Holloway Road, on route 35 to Forest Hill via the Kingsway Subway on 20 January 1952. The subway routes were the last tram services to head into north London and were converted as part of the penultimate stage in the post-war abandonment programme over the weekend of 5/6 April 1952.

On 27 February 1938, two 'HR/2' trams – No 156, about to depart, and No 136, having just arrived – are pictured at the Highgate Village terminus of route 11. The origins of the tram service to Highgate Village lay in a 3ft 6in-gauge cable tramway from the Archway Tavern, which opened originally on 29 May 1884; the route – which ran for just under three-quarters of a mile up Highgate Hill – was the first cable tramway in Europe. The cable tramway survived for 25 years until, in 1909, it was acquired by London and Middlesex county councils; operation ceased in August 1909 and, eight months later, a new standard-gauge electric tramway to Highgate Village opened. Route 11, which linked Highgate Village with Moorgate by the date of conversion, became trolleybus route No 611 on 10 December 1939; its

conversion was delayed as a result of difficulties in establishing a turning circle at Highgate. The replacement trolleybuses were fitted with coasting and run-back brakes – a necessary precaution for operation on Highgate Hill.

NORTH FINCHLEY

Although plans had been in place for the rearrangement of track at Tally Ho! Corner in North Finchley for a number of years, it was not until late 1931 that a comprehensive plan for a new one-way system incorporating a tramway station was completed. Work, however, did not commence until late 1933 and the new layout – as illustrated by 'E/1' No 1074, entering Great North Road with a service on route 9 towards Moorgate – was brought into use in three stages: on 4 and 20 January 1935 and 24 February 1935. The work undertaken here was the most significant trackwork north of the Thames by the LPTB, but it was to have a relatively short life, as the final tram services to North Finchley ceased overnight on 5/6 March 1938. No 1074 was not to last much longer, being scrapped in February 1939.

In 1935, 'Feltham' No 2107 – ex-MET No 363 – stands at the North Finchley terminus of route 45 prior to heading via Finchley and Golders Green to Cricklewood. This service was to become trolleybus service 645 on 2 August 1936. No 2107 was transferred south of the river and was to remain operational until Stage 2 of 'Operation Tramaway' over the weekend of 6/7 January 1951. Sold to Leeds, it became No 541 when it entered service in the West Riding during March 1951. It remained in service for a further five years before withdrawal in October 1956; it was scrapped in September 1957.

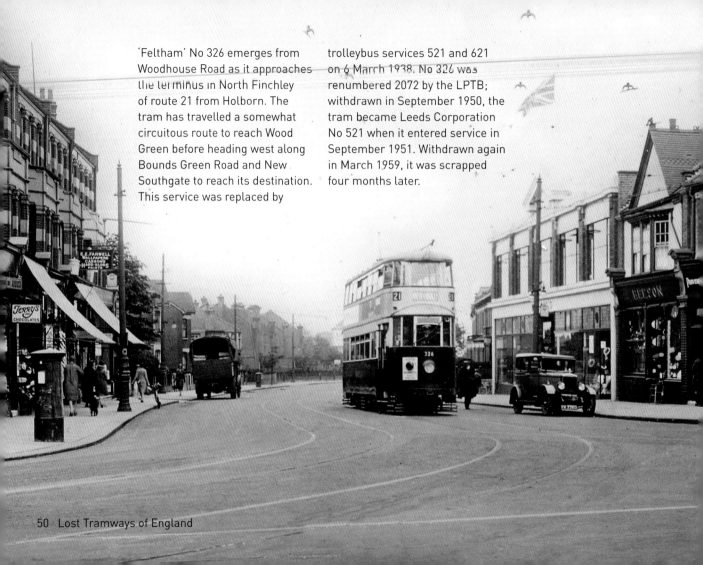

'Feltham' No 326 emerges from Woodhouse Road as it approaches the terminus in North Finchley of route 21 from Holborn. The tram has travelled a somewhat circuitous route to reach Wood Green before heading west along Bounds Green Road and New Southgate to reach its destination. This service was replaced by trolleybus services 521 and 621 on 6 March 1938. No 326 was renumbered 2072 by the LPTB; withdrawn in September 1950, the tram became Leeds Corporation No 521 when it entered service in September 1951. Withdrawn again in March 1959, it was scrapped four months later.

With Barnet church in the background, ex-MET Class H No 2249 stands at the terminus of route 19 to Tottenham Court Road. There were a total of 86 of the type – Nos 2169-254 – in service with the LPTB; of these, 80 were trams that had originally been delivered between 1910 and 1912. These were either built by Brush or by the MET itself using parts supplied by Brush. All had fully enclosed upper-deck top covers fitted from new. The remaining six were rebuilt from damaged older cars during 1924 and 1925. Of the 86, 37 received – as shown by No 249 here – enclosed lower-deck platform vestibules during the late 1920s. The final examples of the type were withdrawn in November 1938; No 2249 was scrapped in October that year.

As a Country Area bus heads outbound, a 'G' class tram – No 2275 – is pictured heading under the LNER branch line to High Barnet, just south of High Barnet station, with an inbound service on route 19 towards Tottenham Court Road. Although undated, the view must date towards the end of the tram service, as the overhead for the replacement trolleybuses is in place. No 2275 was one of 21 of the type; of these 20 – Nos 2262-81 – were originally open-top when delivered from Brush in 1909 and fitted with Mountain & Gibson maximum traction bogies. All were equipped with fully enclosed upper-deck top covers between 1928 and 1930, with enclosed lower-deck vestibules being fitted after 1931. The other member of the class – No 2261 – had been built by MET as an open-top tram in 1921 and underwent the same rebuilding as the other 20 trams. All were withdrawn during 1938, with No 2275 being scrapped in December that year.

Pictured on Cricklewood Broadway towards the end of its life is ex-LUT Class WT No 2409. This was one of five 'W' class trams – LUT Nos 157, 161, 211, 243 and 261 – that were rebuilt in 1928 to incorporate an open-balcony top cover similar in design to those fitted to the LUT's 'T' class. No 2409 had originally been LUT No 243 and was to survive until being scrapped in August 1936. Route 64 operated from Cricklewood to Edgware on weekdays only; the only daily service that operated along Cricklewood Broadway was the 66 from Acton to Canons Park. The latter was the first to be converted, with trolleybuses on route 666 replacing it on 5 July 1936. Just over six weeks later – on 23 August – the 64 was converted into trolleybus service 664 and extended to Paddington (thus converting a peak-hour-only extension into an all-day service).

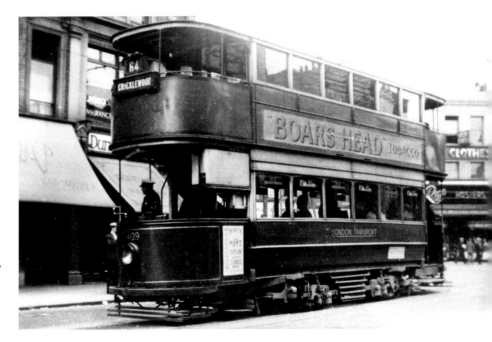

CANONS PARK

On 11 March 1935, ex-LUT 'U' class No 2400 stands at the terminus of route 66 at Canons Park prior to heading inbound along Edgware Road to Acton. The section from Cricklewood to Canons Park was the first of the erstwhile MET network to be converted; the section south from Edgware became trolleybus service 666 on 5 July 1936, with the extension of the route between Edgware and Canons Park being replaced by motorbuses. No 2400 had originally been LUT 'U' class No 297 and was scrapped in July 1936 at Hendon depot.

Pictured in 1935 at the Paddington terminus – located at the junction of Harrow Road and Edgware Road – of route 62 is ex-MET Class A No 2418 in MET livery, albeit now with 'London Transport' along the side panels. A total of 60 of the type – MET Nos 71-130 – were built as open-top bogie cars by Brush in 1904; of these, 55 passed to the LPTB in July 1933, by which date all had been fitted with the enclosed top covers, as carried by No 2418 (originally MET No 81) in this view. The conversion of the ex-MET network to trolleybus operation rendered the type redundant and all were scrapped by the end of 1936; No 2418 was amongst the last to be disposed of, in September that year. Paddington was the terminus of two services that operated each day – the 62 along with the 60 to North Finchley – and the peak-hour-only extension of route 64

from Cricklewood. These services were converted to trolleybus operation in two stages during 1936: on 2 August the 60 became a new 660 service whilst on 23 August the 62 and the 64 became routes 662 and 664 respectively.

Ex-LUT Class U2 No 2405 is pictured at the junction of Craven Park Road and Church Road in Willesden with an outbound service on route 62 towards Stonebridge Park. There were three trams classified 'U2'; these were Nos 2403-05, which had originally been LUT Class W Nos 155, 199 and 288. These three were fitted with new top covers and had altered staircases with a 90° turn; the latter modification permitted the door to the upper saloon to be offset, thus reducing the draught. All three were scrapped in August 1936. Route 62, from Paddington to Sudbury, became trolleybus route 662 on 23 August 1936. Church Road, which headed north from Craven Park, was used by routes 60 (Paddington to North Finchley), 64 (a peak-hour-only extension from Cricklewood to Paddington) and the 66 from Acton to Edgware.

SUDBURY

In April 1933, just prior to the creation of the LPTB, MET No 4 stands at the terminus of route 62 in Sudbury prior to heading inbound with a service on route 62 towards Paddington. In 1904, MET took delivery of 70 Brush-built open-top trams – Classes B and B/1 Nos 1-70 – that were fitted with the same supplier's reversed maximum traction bogies. Between 1912 and 1916, 16 of the type – including No 4 – were fitted at Hendon Works with open-balcony top covers; these were redesignated as Class B2. The balcony ends were originally fitted with wrought iron grilles but this was replaced by sheet metal – as shown here – in about 1931. All 16 passed to LPTB in July 1933 and were renumbered – not wholly in sequence – Nos 2467-82. All were withdrawn during 1935 and 1936 and subsequently scrapped. The 62 was replaced by trolleybus service 662 on 23 August 1936.

In 1929, LUT No 332 stands at the terminus at Shepherds Bush with a service heading towards Southall; the tram shows route 7A – this was a short working of the longer route 7 (prior to 1924 this had been service 87). This tram was one of a batch of 40 – Nos 301-40 – that were built by the United Electric Car Co Ltd on Brill 22E bogies. The type was classified either T/1 or T/2 according to the electrical equipment with which they were fitted. The entire batch was reconditioned during 1925 and passed to the LPTB as Class T in July 1933, being renumbered 2318-57. All were scrapped between July and December 1936; No 332, which became LPTB No 2348, was disposed of during August that year. Shepherds Bush was the terminus of three daily services; these were the 7, which operated westwards along Uxbridge Road to Southall

and Uxbridge, as well as the 57 (to Hounslow) and the 63 to Kew Bridge, both of which operated via Goldhawk Road. The services along Goldhawk Road were replaced by trolleybuses on 27 October 1935 whilst the 7 became trolleybus service 607 on 15 November 1936.

Pictured with Southall Town Hall as the backdrop, LUT No 336 – one of the batch of 40 built in 1914 – awaits departure with a service to Shepherds Bush on route 87; this route number was allocated in 1914 but the service was renumbered in 1924 to become 7A. No 336 was renumbered 2352 by the LPTB and was one of the batch to be scrapped during December 1936. Southall Town Hall was designed by Thomas Newall and completed in 1898 as the home of Southall-Norwood Urban District Council. It remained in local authority use until the creation of the enlarged London Borough of Ealing and has had a number of uses subsequently. The building, which is unlisted (except as a local heritage asset), still stands.

Although the sections of tramway in Hammersmith and Shepherds Bush were within the LCC area, these were initially built and operated by the LUT. It was not until 2 May 1922 that the ownership of these sections was transferred to the LCC, although operation remained in the hands of the LUT. Pictured unloading passengers at Hammersmith in 1929 is 'U' class No 267; this had originally been delivered as an open-top car but had been subsequently fitted with an enclosed top cover. No 267 was to become LPTB No 2374 and was scrapped in July 1936. All of the surviving 'U' class trams were withdrawn following the conversion of routes 57 (Shepherds Bush to Hounslow) and 67 (Hammersmith to Hampton Court) to trolleybus routes 657 and 667 on 27 October 1935. The relatively short route 89 linked Hammersmith with Acton; this service was replaced by trolleybus service 660 on 5 April 1936.

The terminus of routes 26 and 63 was situated on a stub off Chiswick High Road, adjacent to the Star & Garter pub on the north side of the bridge itself. This view, taken in 1925, records LUT No 287 in the foreground prior to departure with a service towards Shepherds Bush on route 63. The second tram visible is an LCC car on route 26 towards London Bridge via Putney Bridge and Wandsworth. No 287 was one of a batch of 150 trams, originally designated Class W by the LUT, that were built by G. F. Milnes & Co (Nos 151-211/37-300) or by British Electric Car Co (Nos 212-36); all were fitted with Brill 22E bogies. A number were fitted with enclosed top covers during 1911 and 1912 and a further batch were modified between 1923 and 1929 using top covers reused from withdrawn trams in the 1-100 batch. The modified trams were classified as Class U and 45 were to pass to the LPTB – as Nos 2358-402 – in July

1933. No 287 became LPTB No 2392 and was scrapped in July 1936. Route 26 was cut back to Hammersmith on 26 October 1935; the following day saw the 63 replaced by trolleybuses operating on routes 657 and 667.

The short route 55 from Hanwell to Brentford along Boston Road was operated for a period by four single-deck trams, Nos 341-44. This was the result of a visit by Charles J. Spencer and other officers from the tramway to the USA during 1919. There the group experienced the use of single-deck one-man operated trams on lightly trafficked routes and, on their return, it was decided to try out similar vehicles on London routes. No 341, pictured here on Boston Road, had originally been MET No 132 and was sold, after conversion at Hendon, to the LUT. It was initially tested on the route from Richmond Park Gates to Tolworth, which proved unsatisfactory, and, on 14 March 1923, approval was granted for its use on route 55. Three further trams were converted later in 1923. At the same time No 341 was converted from a four-wheel car to operate using Brill 22E bogies. Single-deck operation of route 55 continued until 9 November 1928; the four trams were then stored and were sold for scrap in February 1931.

Although retaining its original LUT livery, 'Feltham' No 2163 has received its LPTB fleet number in this view taken at Uxbridge. Route 7 from Shepherds Bush to Uxbridge was converted to trolleybus service No 607 on 15 November 1936; this was the penultimate ex-LUT service to be converted. No 2163, which had originally been LUT No 394, was seriously damaged in an accident after the war and was scrapped at Purley depot in December 1949.

CREDITS

Lost Tramways of England London North-West. Published in Great Britain in 2021 by Graffeg Limited.

Written by Peter Waller copyright © 2021. Designed and produced by Graffeg Limited copyright © 2021.

Graffeg Limited, 24 Stradey Park Business Centre, Mwrwg Road, Llangennech, Llanelli, Carmarthenshire, SA14 8YP, Wales, UK. Tel: 01554 824000. www.graffeg.com.

Peter Waller is hereby identified as the author of this work in accordance with section 77 of the Copyrights, Designs and Patents Act 1988.

A CIP Catalogue record for this book is available from the British Library.

ISBN 9781914079818

1 2 3 4 5 6 7 8 9

MIX
Paper from responsible sources
FSC® C014138
www.fsc.org

Photo credits

© C. Carter Collection: pages 13, 31.

© Julian Thompson/Online Transport Archive: pages 14, 18, 19, 24, 44.

© Phil Tatt/Online Transport Archive: page 15.

© Ian L. Wright/Online Transport Archive: page 16.

© H. B. Priestley/National Tramway Museum: pages 20, 29, 40.

© W. A. Camwell/National Tramway Museum: pages 22, 23, 27, 39, 43, 47.

© John Meredith Collection/Online Transport Archive: pages 30, 33, 35, 37, 55, 60-62.

© Barry Cross Collection/Online Transport Archive: pages 32, 48, 50-52, 58, 59.

© D. W. K. Jones/National Tramway Museum: pages 34, 41, 49, 54, 56.

© N. D. W. Elston/John Meredith Collection/Online Transport Archive: page 53.

© Maurice O'Connor/National Tramway Museum: page 57.

© Hugh Nicol/National Tramway Museum: page 63.

The photographs used in this book have come from a variety of sources. Wherever possible contributors have been identified although some images may have been used without credit or acknowledgement and if this is the case apologies are offered and full credit will be given in any future edition.

Cover: The Angel, Islington.
Back cover: Rosebery Avenue, Kingsway Subway, Bloomsbury.

Lost Tramways of Wales:
• **Cardiff** ISBN 9781912213122
• **North Wales** ISBN 9781912213139
• **South Wales and Valleys** ISBN 9781912213146
• **Swansea and Mumbles** ISBN 9781912213153

Lost Tramways of England:
• **Birmingham North** ISBN 9781912654390
• **Birmingham South** ISBN 9781912654383
• **Bradford** ISBN 9781912654406
• **Brighton** ISBN 9781912654376
• **Bristol** ISBN 9781912654345
• **Coventry** ISBN 9781912654338
• **Leeds West** ISBN 9781913733506
• **Leeds East** ISBN 9781914079580
• **Nottingham** ISBN 9781912654352
• **Southampton** ISBN 9781912654369
• **London North-East** ISBN 9781914079801
• **London North-West** ISBN 9781914079818
• **London South-East** ISBN 9781914079825
• **London South-West** ISBN 9781914079832

Lost Tramways of Scotland:
• **Aberdeen** ISBN 9781912654413
• **Dundee** ISBN 9781912654420
• **Edinburgh** ISBN 9781913733513
• **Glasgow South** ISBN 9781914079528
• **Glasgow North** ISBN 9781914079542

Lost Tramways of Ireland:
• **Belfast** ISBN 9781914079504